Kevin's Python Coding Coloring Book

By

Kevin Bancroft

Copyright

Dedication

This book dedicated to Grandpa and Grandma Hobkirk.

Acknowledgement

Thanks to Robert Hobkirk for helping me with this book.

Table of Contents

Contents

Epigraph

Chinese Proverb, "A journey of a thousand miles begins with a single step."

Introduction

Hello and welcome to my Python coding coloring book. Today we are going to talk about coding. Python coding is a computer coding language. Code tells the computer what to do. You can do many things with Python, including graphics.

To make these graphics on your computer, first you have to download Python. Download Python from https://www.python.org/downloads/. Be sure to download the proper version for your computer and operating system.

After you have downloaded Python, run it, and a Python shell will appear. You have to click on "File" then "New Window." Use the new window screen to enter the code, then click on "Run." It will prompt you with "Save." After saving, it will run. This book has one page for the picture to be colored, and on the other page is the code used to create it. You can make your own designs by tweaking the code with changing the numbers.

Have Fun!

Coding And Pictures

```
import turtle
t = turtle.Pen()
for x in range(5):
    t.circle(120)
    t.left(72)
```

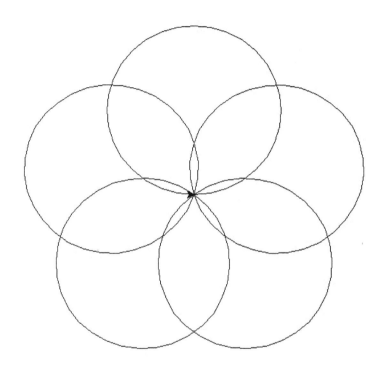

```
import turtle
t = turtle.Pen()
for x in range(10):
    t.circle(120)
    t.left(200)
```

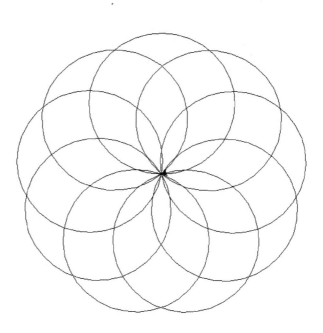

```
import turtle
t = turtle.Pen()
for x in range(30):
    t.circle(120)
    t.left(50)
```

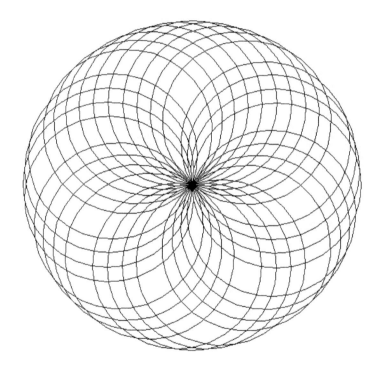

```python
import turtle
t = turtle.Pen()
for x in range(40):
    t.circle(120)
    t.left(9)
```

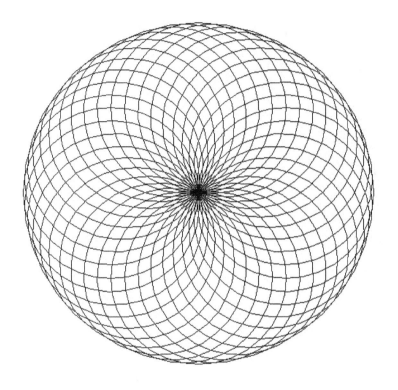

```python
import turtle
t = turtle.Pen()
for x in range(20):
    t.circle(120)
    t.left(9)
```

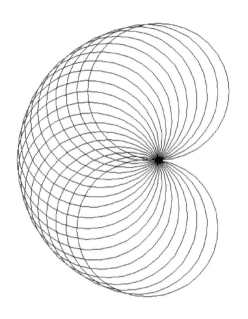

```
import turtle
t = turtle.Pen()
for x in range(200):
    t.forward(x)
    t.right(75)
```

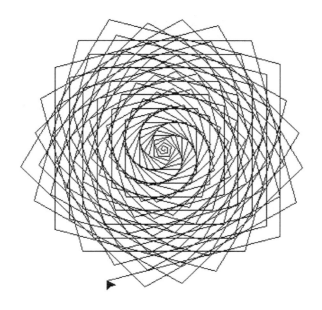

```
import turtle
t = turtle.Pen()
for x in range(200):
    t.forward(x)
    t.right(30)
```

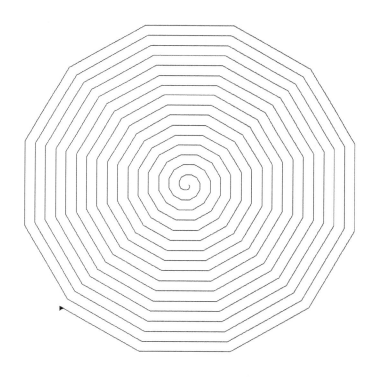

21

```
import turtle
t = turtle.Pen()
for x in range(300):
    t.forward(x)
    t.left(122)
```

```
import turtle
t = turtle.Pen()
for x in range(300):
    t.forward(x)
    t.left(99)
```

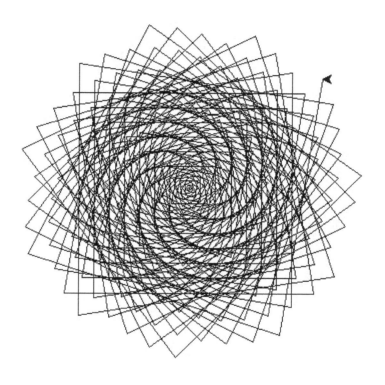

```
import turtle
t = turtle.Pen()
for x in range(300):
    t.forward(x)
    t.left(230)
import turtle
t = turtle.Pen()
for x in range(6):
    t.circle(100)
    t.left(60)
```

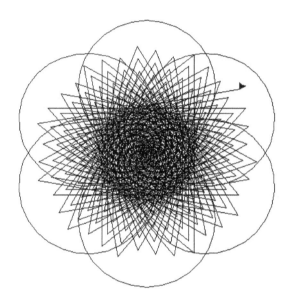

```python
import turtle
t = turtle.Pen()
for x in range(300):
    t.forward(x)
    t.left(270)
```

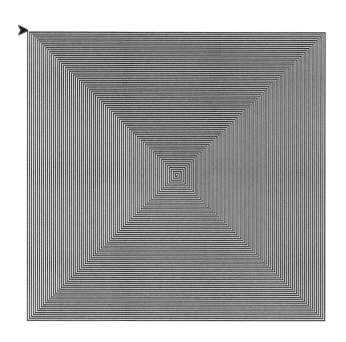

```
import turtle
t = turtle.Pen()
for x in range(11):
    t.circle(100)
    t.left(86)
```

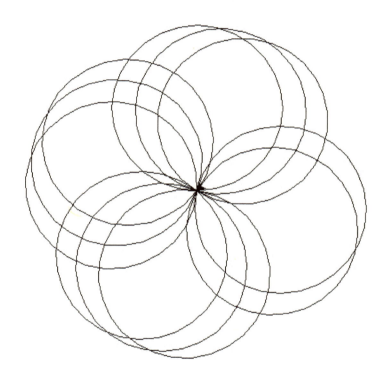

```python
import turtle
t = turtle.Pen()
for x in range(250):
    t.forward(x)
    t.left(150)
```

33

```
import turtle
t = turtle.Pen()
for x in range(300):
    t.forward(x)
    t.left(195)
```

About the Author

Hello, my name is Kevin Bancroft. I like doing stuff on computers. I code and make graphics. I like to play video games. I was learning python during the summer, and I thought it would be fun to make a coloring book by making designs using code. Maybe I will do another book in the future if I get any new ideas.

www.ingramcontent.com/pod-product-compliance
Lightning Source LLC
Chambersburg PA
CBHW051217050326
40689CB00008B/1351